POLES AND GRIDWORK

by

Jane Wallace

Illustrations by

Carole Vincer

THRESHOLD BOOKS

First published in Great Britain by
Threshold Books, The Kenilworth Press Limited,
Addington, Buckingham, MK18 2JR

British Library Cataloguing in Publication Data
A catalogue record for this book is available from the British Library.

ISBN 1-872082-44-0

Typeset by The Kenilworth Press Limited

Printed in Great Britain by Westway Offset, Wembley

CONTENTS ■ ■ ■ ■ ■ ■ ■ ■ ■ ■ ■ ■ ■ ■ ■

Introduction

Poles on the ground and grids of small fences are useful for introducing a young horse to jumping and for providing suppling exercises for novice and more experienced horses alike. The exercises described will have a beneficial effect on the horse's flatwork because they will stretch the horse's back and loosen other muscles and joints.

The distances stated in the various grids are approximate. The shorter figure is for ponies and the longer one for horses, but flexibility must be applied to fit individual animals. Base your distances on a horse's average stride being 3.6m (12 ft) and a pony's being 2.7m (9 ft).

Make sure that all the fences are built very small to begin with. Only increase the size when you know the distance is suitable for your horse.

It is essential to have someone on the ground who can help and advise. Never jump on your own in case of an accident.

The pattern for introducing a horse to jumping is the same as for flatwork. The horse must be calm, in rhythm and balanced. If he is tense, his jump will be stiff and unathletic. The approach to the fence will be a problem as well, because the horse will be unable to remain in rhythm and balance.

Grids give the rider an opportunity to perfect his position over a fence. He must remain in balance with a secure lower leg. He must not collapse over his horse's neck while in the air but should control the forward swing of his upper body. His eyes should be looking towards the next fence.

The horse must be allowed freedom of his head and neck over the fence, to balance himself, so the rider must follow with his hand as the horse takes off.

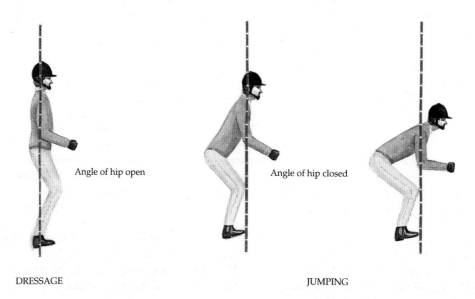

Angle of hip open

Angle of hip closed

DRESSAGE

JUMPING

RIDER'S POSITION

One pole on the ground

This is how you introduce a horse to jumping for the very first time. To start with he should be asked to walk over a single pole. Horses will react in different ways when first presented with a pole on the ground. Some will step over it without a second thought; some will leap over it; others will refuse to tackle the problem. In this latter case, the rider must be firm - certainly not allowing the horse to turn away - and insist that he steps over it somehow. However the horse reacts, he must be rewarded with a pat once he has successfully negotiated the pole.

He should be walked over the pole from both directions and on the angle. Once the horse is happy doing this, he can be asked to do the same in trot - firstly straight, and then on the oblique and off turns. All the time the rider should be thinking of rhythm and balance

with the horse calm and confident. Only when the horse accepts one pole can he progress further.

A single pole on the ground approached in canter is a good exercise for keeping the rhythm. Horses, young and old, benefit from this exercise; so do experienced and inexperienced riders. The rider should take up a forward position and canter round over the pole. The horse should remain in the same shape with the same rhythm and should neither quicken nor resist. The rider should keep his eye on the pole and see if he can judge whether the horse is meeting it on the correct stride. If he sees the horse is going to get too close to the pole, he can close his hand to shorten the stride, or soften the hand to lengthen the stride, as necessary. It is a good exercise for judging distances.

Trotting poles

The horse has to lift his legs higher to clear the poles

1.2 - 1.5m (4 - 5ft)

A natural progression from a single pole on the ground is a line of trotting poles. These should be placed 1.2 - 1.5m (4 - 5ft) apart, depending on the horse or pony's length of stride. The horse should not have to reach for the poles nor have to shorten his stride.

The extra poles should be introduced gradually, especially for the young horse. Do not suddenly present him with a long line; build up to a maximum of six, one at a time.

Keep the basic principles in mind as you work your horse over the poles: calmness, forward movement, rhythm and balance. The poles will help improve these as well as increasing suppleness. The horse has to lift his legs higher to clear the poles, so exercising his knees, hocks, fetlocks, stifles and shoulders.

The rider should maintain a light contact and in no way restrict the horse, either on the approach or over the poles. The horse does not need to over-stretch his neck over the poles but should be allowed to carry himself in balance. The rider should remain in rising trot to allow the horse's back to swing. Sitting trot may cause the back to stiffen and minimum weight should be on the back to encourage it to be supple.

The poles can be approached from some distance away or can be turned into from a turn. You could use them as part of a figure-of-eight exercise so that you change the direction each time. This helps improve the suppleness, because the horse will have used his hocks over the poles and will be more ready to carry himself on the corner afterwards.

If the horse should try to alter rhythm or pace on the approach, the rider should correct this with half-halts.

Lungeing over trotting poles

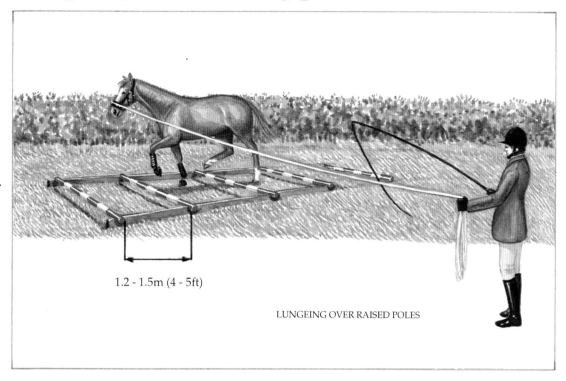

1.2 - 1.5m (4 - 5ft)

LUNGEING OVER RAISED POLES

A useful exercise for suppling the horse is to lunge him over poles. Trotting poles, placed on a circle 1.2 - 1.5m (4 - 5ft) apart in the centre, up to six in number, encourage the horse to use himself to the full and improve rhythm and balance. Without the rider's weight, the horse has no restriction of any sort and has to sort out the poles for himself.

If the horse carries himself naturally in a good outline, it is ideal not to have any side-reins, but if the horse carries his head high in the air, some loose side-reins should encourage him to work in a rounder outline. The side-reins must not be tight, otherwise the horse will stiffen in his back over the poles.

Later on in a horse's training - i.e. with a mature horse - he can be asked to work over raised trotting poles. The poles can be raised a few inches by using two pieces of planking with notches cut at the necessary distance. The extra height makes the horse work much harder because he has to lift his legs quite high to clear the poles. The first pole should be on the ground so that if he misjudges it he will not fall flat on his face!

The horse should not wear side-reins when working over raised poles because he needs maximum freedom of his head and neck to keep his balance.

Trotting poles help teach a horse to look what he is doing, and raised poles will make him respect poles all the more. Raised poles are a tiring exercise for the horse and should not be used for long periods. It depends on the fitness of the horse, but you will soon see if your horse is getting tired. You should then stop.

Canter poles on a circle

Four poles are placed on the ground at the quarter points of a 20-metre circle. The horse is asked first to trot round over the poles and then to repeat the exercise in canter.

This exercise is good practice for both horse and rider. For the horse it teaches him to look what he is doing, and it helps to improve his rhythm and balance. For the rider it teaches rhythm and distance, and makes him look ahead to the next 'fence'.

Many riders fall into the bad habit of looking down over their fences. If the rider looks down in this exercise, he will be unable to judge where to jump the next pole and whether he needs to make any adjustment to the stride pattern.

In the same way that you look over the handlebars when riding a bike, or look ahead when driving a car, so you must look in the direction you are going when riding a horse. Your eyes will guide you in the correct direction and you will automatically give the necessary aid. This is crucial when jumping a course of fences. Unless you look towards the next fence in a course you will not find the correct line to each fence. It should be automatic to look ahead over a fence.

If the horse makes a mistake at a pole and breaks into trot, the rider should ask him to strike off into canter as he steps over the next pole.

Quick reactions are important when riding, and in particular when jumping, and this exercise offers a good test of speed of reaction to loss of rhythm and picking it up again quickly.

Repeat this exercise on both reins.

Cantering over a small fence

This is a continuation from cantering over a single pole on the ground and the previous exercise on the circle. The fence need only be 45cm (18ins) high with a ground pole on either side, the same distance away as the height of the fence. This makes it an easy, inviting fence to jump.

Exactly the same principles should be adhered to when jumping this raised pole as when jumping a pole on the ground. The horse must remain calm, in rhythm, with forward movement and impulsion. The horse can then lengthen and shorten his stride with ease should he need to do so.

The horse should arrive in the approach in a balanced canter in an unrestricted outline. If the horse feels any restriction from the rider, it will make him feel that he must increase pace to jump. This becomes a bad habit which is difficult to cure and which will tend to get worse with bigger fences.

The rider should sit lightly in the saddle with his shoulders a little in front of the vertical so that he is ready to go with the horse and remain in balance. A tiny fence such as this does not need the rider to be 'in behind his horse' as some cross-country fences demand.

The rider should concentrate on keeping the rhythm and balance all the way to take-off, and remain in balance himself. The worst mistake is to get in front of your horse, thereby altering his balance on the approach. In the same way that dressage should look easy and harmonious, so jumping should appear the same. By practising over tiny fences and poles, this should not be difficult to achieve. The rider simply has to apply the same principles when jumping bigger fences.

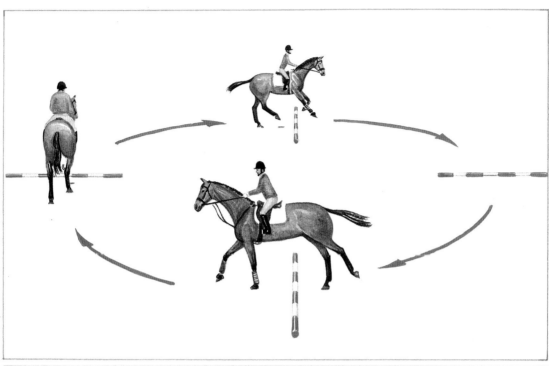

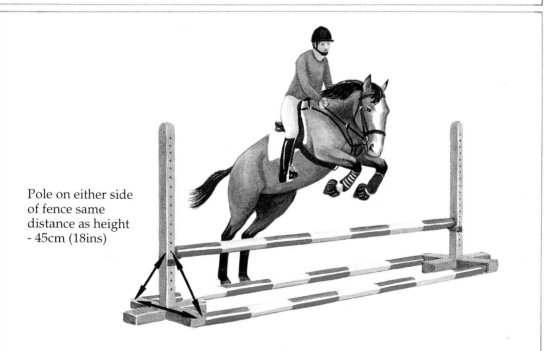

Pole on either side
of fence same
distance as height
- 45cm (18ins)

Introducing a grid

Before a horse is asked to work through a grid, he should be made familiar with the positioning of a placing pole in front of a simple fence. This trot pole (you should approach in trot) places the horse in the correct spot for take-off. If the horse does not understand how to cope with this pole, any future grid exercise will be adversely affected.

The trot pole should be placed 1.8 - 2.7m (6 - 9ft) away from a cross-pole. This means that the horse should jump the pole and then jump the fence. If the horse trots over the pole, he will not meet the fence well.

On the approach, the rider must concentrate on keeping the horse balanced, going forward, straight and in a rhythm. He should keep his legs closed around the horse and squeeze him as he gets to the pole to encourage him to jump it. On no account should he alter his body position or send the horse flat by pushing him onto his forehand at the last minute.

Always remember when jumping that it is the horse that jumps the fence, not the rider. Do not try to influence the jump with your body.

The purpose of a cross-pole is to keep the horse to the middle of the fence. It is important that the horse is conditioned always to jump the centre of his fences. It is up to the rider to present his horse correctly.

When the horse becomes proficient at coping with this exercise, the fence can be built straight, with a ground line 30 - 60cm (1 - 2ft) away. It is a useful method of encouraging a horse to jump from his hocks and use himself. It helps the rider feel rhythm and balance.

Trotting poles to a cross-pole

Three or four trotting poles placed 1.2 - 1.5m (4 - 5ft) apart can be used to precede a cross-pole. A distance of 2.1 - 2.7m (7 - 9ft) should be set between the final pole and the cross-pole. This is an excellent exercise for teaching the rider about rhythm and balance before a fence. If the rider in any way alters the horse's balance or rhythm by trying to push the horse into the fence, the horse will be unable to do the exercise. There is room for another stride of trot in between the last pole and the fence, but the horse will not be able to fit in that stride if pushed out of rhythm or balance. Any movement of the rider's upper body will affect the horse and it is indeed a most revealing test.

Having learned in trot to preserve the precious feeling of true balance and rhythm, coupled with forward movement, the same can be done when approaching a fence in canter. All too often one sees riders hurling their horses at jumps, increasing pace and losing balance in the last few strides. This is when it is so vitally important to keep everything - rhythm, balance, impulsion and rider's position - the same.

The rider should approach this exercise in rising trot with the angle of the hip closed in readiness for jumping the fence at the end. He should look at the first pole until it disappears beneath the horse's ears. He should then look at the fence, feeling the same trot rhythm over the poles, in between the poles and up to the fence itself. It is important that the rider never gets in front of the movement and 'jumps' the fence before the horse. This exercise will expose this fault.

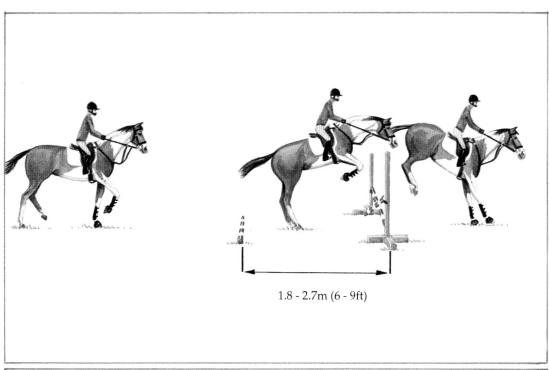

1.8 - 2.7m (6 - 9ft)

Poles 1.2 - 1.5m
(4 - 5ft) apart

2.1 - 2.7m (7 - 9ft)

Cross-pole to parallel

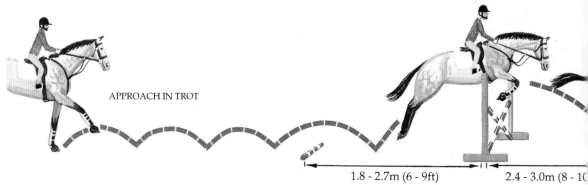

APPROACH IN TROT

1.8 - 2.7m (6 - 9ft)   2.4 - 3.0m (8 - 1(

This is the most simple of grids. It builds upon the trot pole to cross-pole exercise by adding a pole on the ground 2.4 - 3.0m (8 - 10ft) away, with a small parallel the same distance away.

The purpose of this grid is to teach a horse good technique. The trot pole and cross-pole are to set him up and put him at the correct take-off point for the parallel. In order to clear the spread and yet not touch the front pole, the horse must lift his knees and shoulders, and fold his forelegs as well as 'open out' behind. This means that he must not cramp his hind legs underneath him but lift them up and out.

This exercise should be of small dimensions for a novice horse but can be made quite demanding for an older, more experienced horse. It is a useful exercise

Trotting poles to cross-pole to parallel

This is a variation on the above grid. Instead, there are four trotting poles on the approach, the last one 2.1 - 2.7m (7 - 9ft) away from the cross-pole. There is then a parallel 4.5 - 5.4m (15 - 18ft) away. Because the distance between the cross-pole and the parallel is longer, there is no need for the extra ground pole in between.

The difference between these two grids is that the horse is more likely to arrive balanced in this grid due to the line of poles. The rider knows he has to sit still, whereas in the previous grid there is a temptation to encourage the horse to jump the first pole by moving the upper body. With this exercise, any movement of the upper body will be exposed over the initial poles.

It is important that the rider makes

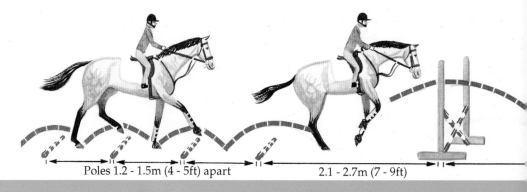

Poles 1.2 - 1.5m (4 - 5ft) apart   2.1 - 2.7m (7 - 9ft)

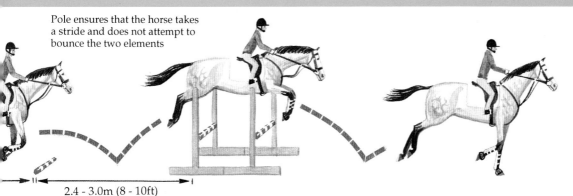

Pole ensures that the horse takes a stride and does not attempt to bounce the two elements

2.4 - 3.0m (8 - 10ft)

for any standard of horse. It is also a good test for a rider.

The rider must be able to keep his position throughout by keeping the weight well in the heel, the seat low, head and eyes up and shoulders not collapsed over the horse's neck. He must allow the horse to use his head and neck to the full.

The rider should approach the exercise in a forward-going, balanced, rhythmical trot. He should keep his legs closed around the horse but allow the horse to do the jumping. He must allow the horse to jump up underneath him, and not force the horse's shoulders down by swinging forward too soon or overmuch.

Make sure you pick up the rhythm immediately when you ride away from the grid.

miminum movement with his body through the exercise. He must allow the horse's jump to fold him at the hips (but not too much) and then he should hold this position until the exercise is finished. If the rider bends too much at the first element, then he will have to straighten up in between. This excess movement will be unbalancing for the horse and may cause him to hit the second element.

This exercise is good practice for learning to sit as still as possible. This is what a rider must do in a combination or double to give his horse maximum chance of clearing it. All too often one sees excess body swing causing a horse to hit fences, particularly in related distances. The position of the rider is therefore all-important, as it can either help or hinder the horse.

4.5 - 5.4m (15 - 18ft)

Simple grid with vertical

This is an extension of the basic exercise of cross-pole to parallel. These are then followed by a vertical (upright) on two short strides at a distance of 7.2 - 9.6m (24 - 32ft). The vertical should have a ground pole approximately 60cm (2ft) away to help the horse 'back off' (shorten his stride just before take-off to help him spring in the air).

The principles of riding this exercise are the same as the previous ones. The rider should allow the horse to jump the fences and jump up under him. He must sit as still as possible with minimal upper body movement. He must try not to influence the horse's stride pattern in between the parallel and the upright, but try merely to maintain rhythm and balance.

If the horse is losing impulsion, he should close his leg (but keep his body still), and if the horse should try to quicken, he should keep his leg still and close his hand. If the rider loses position over the top of a fence, he will involuntarily move his leg on landing which may well give the horse an aid to quicken. The more sensitive the horse, the more important it is that the rider has full control of his lower leg and position.

It is very important that the rider never balances on his hand. This is a bad fault and the horse will react adversely to it.

The whole exercise should be done with minimum fuss. If carried out with rhythm, balance and impulsion, the performance should look effortless and easy. It may be necessary to lengthen the distance if the fences are bigger. It is important to start with low fences so that if the distance does not suit your horse, he will not be worried. Low fences forgive mistakes.

Simple grid with parallel

This is identical to the previous grid except that there is a parallel at 7.2 - 9.6m (24 - 32ft) instead of a vertical. You can vary this further by replacing the trot pole with a line of trotting poles - in fact, all these grids can be adapted as you wish. There are many different variations on the same theme; these are just a few suggestions and ideas.

The parallel at the end of the line puts great emphasis on the horse's technique. It is not necessary to have a ground line in front of this fence, but the front pole should have the ground line directly beneath it. The parallel is sufficiently imposing to back off the horse, whereas an upright fence is more difficult for a horse to judge, so he needs help from a ground pole, particularly if he is a youngster.

The rider must concentrate on holding his position throughout the exercise. The bigger the horse jumps, the more difficult it can be to keep the heels down. Parallels will make a horse jump with more effort, and the rider will have to work hard to sit correctly.

As with other grids, this one should start very small and gradually be built up to a size fitting to the level of the horse's and rider's training. It is imperative **never to overface your horse**. Obviously it is easier to jump bigger fences at the end of a line, because the distances are set and there is no chance of the horse being 'wrong' for take-off. However, fences do not need to be big to make horses use themselves. Always have an experienced person on the ground to advise. This will help avoid any problems.

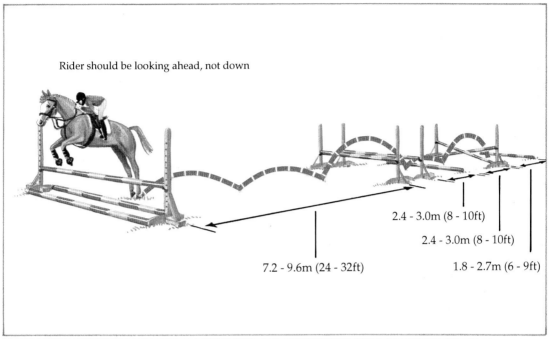

Rider should be looking ahead, not down

2.4 - 3.0m (8 - 10ft)

2.4 - 3.0m (8 - 10ft)

7.2 - 9.6m (24 - 32ft)

1.8 - 2.7m (6 - 9ft)

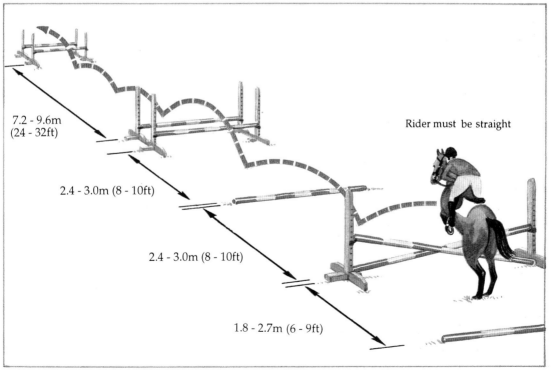

7.2 - 9.6m
(24 - 32ft)

Rider must be straight

2.4 - 3.0m (8 - 10ft)

2.4 - 3.0m (8 - 10ft)

1.8 - 2.7m (6 - 9ft)

Introducing bounces

Bounces are useful athletic and suppling exercises for horse and rider. A bounce varies in distance from 3.0 - 4.5m (10 - 15ft) depending on the size and siting of the fences. In an exercise when the fences are small, the shorter distances will be more suitable. If you start with the fences tiny, you will be able to adjust the distances to suit your horse or pony without causing problems. If the distances are incorrect for your horse and you set off down a sizeable grid, your horse will struggle to jump through. This may worry him and make him lose confidence. If the fences are 45cm (18ins) high, you cannot frighten any horse.

Use a trot pole as a placing pole to introduce the horse to the grid, then put your bounce 1.8 - 2.7m (6 - 9ft) away, placing the two cross-poles 3.0 - 3.6m (10 - 12ft) apart. The cross-pole keeps the horse in the centre of the fences and holds him straight as he bounces. A possible fault is for the horse to jump crooked over the second element, so the cross prevents this.

The rider's position is important. It is vital that he does not collapse over his horse's neck in a bounce (he shouldn't over any fence, but must take extra care to avoid doing so over a bounce fence). In order for the horse to spring into the air to jump the second or maybe third element, he must be light on his forehand. If the rider's weight is too far forward it will be all the more difficult for the horse to take off. The rider must keep the weight in his heel and his head up, and he must keep a contact throughout. The horse will need the support of his rider's hand through a bounce. Balance is all-important.

Double bounce to upright

This is an extension of the above exercise. Here the horse must do a double bounce, then take one stride and jump another fence 4.5 - 5.4m (15 - 18ft) away. This tests and improves the horse's athletic ability and speeds up his reactions. For the rider it is a good test of balance.

The trot pole helps the horse arrive at the correct take-off point. The rider must ensure that the horse is balanced and in a good rhythm with impulsion.

Bear in mind that you must not drop the contact, but follow with the hand; that you must not fling your upper body forward, but allow the horse's jump to close the angle of the hip to form the forward swing; and that you should present the horse at the grid and allow him to jump it. Do not try to influence the jump with your body or by 'lifting' the horse with your hand. Keep as still as possible to help the horse adjust his balance as he lands and takes off. Most riders move their body too much when jumping bounces. The stiller you sit, the easier it will be for the horse. Imagine how difficult it is to give a 'piggy-back' to someone who is wriggling around!

To test that the horse is jumping straight, the cross-poles can be changed but the rider must make sure that he does not allow the horse to drift to one side. The final element gives the horse an easier jump by allowing him to take a stride. Bounce fences are found on most event courses so it is important to master them. Do not practise over them too often, though - perhaps every other time when the horse is working through grids. Variation is important when schooling.

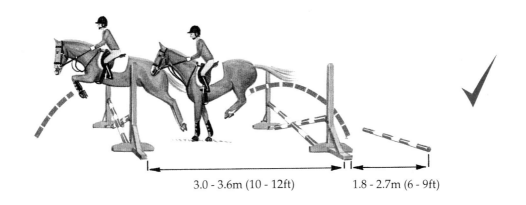

3.0 - 3.6m (10 - 12ft)   1.8 - 2.7m (6 - 9ft)

Rider must have a secure seat with the weight in the heel

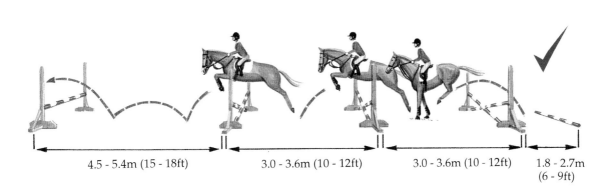

4.5 - 5.4m (15 - 18ft)   3.0 - 3.6m (10 - 12ft)   3.0 - 3.6m (10 - 12ft)   1.8 - 2.7m (6 - 9ft)

Bounces from canter

3.0 - 4.5m (10 - 15ft)   3.0 - 4.5m (10 - 15ft)

This is an exercise jumped from canter. It can be built very small initially and then increased to suit the standard of horse and rider. It is useful to jump some exercises from canter because a grid is only a means to an end and eventually you have to jump out of canter. A distance of 3.0 - 4.5m (10 - 15ft) should be suitable for most horses and ponies but the distance can be altered if necessary. The exercise should appear easy for the horse and there should be no obvious altering of stride, rhythm or balance.

The distance in between the elements affects the pace of canter on the approach. The longer the distances, the stronger the pace can be. It is important to judge the pace required for the different distances so that you can meet your fences correctly when riding in competition across country. All too often you see riders approaching bounces much too fast,

Grid layout 1

Poles 1.2m - 1.5m (4 - 5ft) apart   2.1 - 2.7m (7 - 9ft)   4.5 - 5.4m (15 - 18ft)

This is a more complicated grid which provides variation and increased difficulty. It may be built very small to suit the novice horse and rider or it may be constructed with more demanding heights for experienced combinations. Four trotting poles are set out 1.2 - 1.5m (4 - 5ft) apart followed by an upright 2.1 - 2.7m (7 - 9ft) away. (Much depends on the pony's length of stride. If the trotting poles need to be closer together to fit the stride, the distance to the upright should be reduced.) Another upright should be set up 4.5 - 5.4m (15 - 18ft) away and then a parallel 4.8 - 5.7m (16 - 19ft) further on. There should be a ground pole at all three fences to back off the horse and so prevent him getting too close for take-off.

The exercise is a good test of balance and rhythm. The rider must ensure that he arrives in the centre of the trotting

4.8 - 5.7m (16 - 19ft)   4.8 - 5.7m (16 - 19ft)

resulting in the horse struggling to shorten himself to negotiate the bounce successfully. It is therefore important to practise these types of fence at home so that you are confident about how to ride them.

The canter on the approach must be bouncy, full of impulsion with rhythm and balance. The rider must remain in balance throughout, holding a correct position and not making undue

movement with his upper body. He must keep the contact with the horse's mouth, but without causing any restriction which may cause the horse to hollow and lose athleticism. The horse must be allowed to use his head and neck to the full, for balance. The rider should practise changing from a strong, simulated cross-country pace to a pace suitable for a bounce.

4.8 - 5.7m (16 - 19ft)

poles and that his horse is straight. There is no cross-pole to keep the horse in the middle this time, so it is up to the rider. The horse must be in a good rhythm and be well balanced with impulsion. This must be preserved throughout the exercise. The horse must not lose impulsion but at the same time the rider must not hurry his horse. The horse should jump deliberately and slowly and not whizz through flat-out.

The rider must concentrate on keeping his position. He must stay in balance and not get in front of his horse at the point of take-off. He should keep his head up and look towards the final element. Weight must be in the heel so that he can allow the horse freedom without losing security of seat.

This is an excellent exercise.

Grid layout 2

Another variation on the same theme: two trotting poles are followed by a cross-pole at 2.1 - 2.7m (7 - 9ft); 4.5 - 5.4m (15 - 18ft) away is the first parallel; then 4.8 - 5.7m (16 - 19ft) further on is a second parallel; which is followed by 7.2 - 9.0m (24 - 30ft) to an upright. This tests the horse's technique by opening him up over two parallels, then asking him to jump an upright off a short stride. All these fences (except the cross-pole) should have ground poles and the ground pole for the upright fence should be 60cm (2ft) away.

If the distances do not seem to suit your horse, you may have to alter them slightly. A long-striding horse may struggle to shorten for the final distance, in which case pull out the upright to make it easier.

This is a good test of athletic ability for the horse. For the rider it tests being able to present the horse in balance and rhythm, and whether he can keep a good position throughout.

The fences must start small and increase in size very gradually. If you make the parallels wider, remember that you will, in effect, be making the distances shorter. (Always walk a distance from the back rail of a parallel to the front rail of the next fence.) An experienced horse will be able to shorten his stride without problem, but a younger horse may find this difficult. Avoid putting the horse in too tight a situation so that he tries to miss out a stride. He may hurt himself or have a fright, both of which must be avoided. If you feel him struggle, alter the distance to help him. A short distance to a wide spread is a test of a horse's scope and ability. This exercise will reveal much about your horse's talent. Beware of making it too difficult.

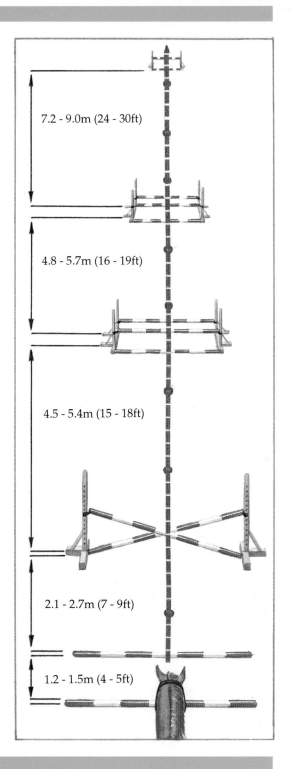

7.2 - 9.0m (24 - 30ft)

4.8 - 5.7m (16 - 19ft)

4.5 - 5.4m (15 - 18ft)

2.1 - 2.7m (7 - 9ft)

1.2 - 1.5m (4 - 5ft)

Jumping on the angle

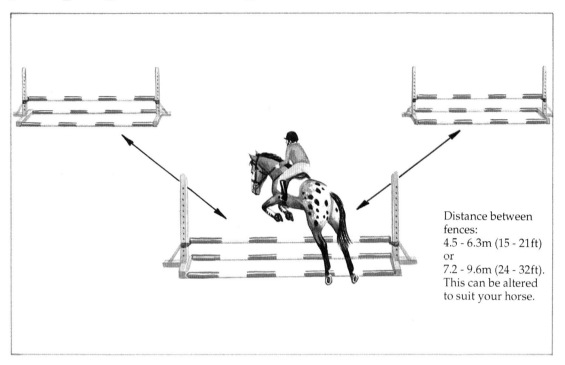

Distance between fences:
4.5 - 6.3m (15 - 21ft)
or
7.2 - 9.6m (24 - 32ft).
This can be altered to suit your horse.

Jumping fences on the angle should be part of the horse's education, but he must not be asked to do this until his training is well-established and he is between hand and leg.

As a basic rule, all fences should be jumped straight and in the middle, but there are times, when jumping against the clock for instance, when the horse may be asked to jump obliquely across a fence to save time.

There is less margin for error when jumping on the angle - the horse may be tempted to run out or drop a leg (leave one foreleg dangling lower than the other on take-off).

It is important that the horse is obedient to the aids and is carrying himself in a balanced way before being asked to jump across a fence. The angle can vary from being a slight deviation from the straight to an acute line across the fence. The higher the level of training, the sharper the angle can be, but accuracy and obedience are vital.

A good exercise for practising jumping on the angle is to set out three fences in a triangle, leaving a distance between related elements of either one or two strides. The distance will depend upon the size of the fences - smaller fences need shorter distances. The distances may range from 4.5 - 6.3m (15 - 21ft) for one stride or 7.2 - 9.6m (24 - 32ft) for two strides. The distance can be changed by jumping the fences to one side or another, so making the distance longer or shorter. If you begin with small fences, you can play with the distances to suit your horse. When jumping from canter, the pace of the canter will alter the distance.

Working at home over fences like this teaches the rider what distances suit his horse and from what pace.

Turning exercise

In order to jump fences on the angle and turn quickly without losing rhythm and balance, horse and rider must practise this at home. Two fences built just off the track can be used as an exercise to teach a horse to jump off either rein. The exercise may be ridden as a figure of eight but should not be used for too long. It is strenuous and tiring and the horse should not be asked to repeat it too often.

Before working over an exercise such as this, make sure that your horse is well warmed up and has been popped over some straightforward fences. Start by jumping just one fence, off the horse's better rein. All horses turn better one way than the other, and although you need to improve the stiff rein, it is important to start with the easier one. Jump the same fence a few times until the horse turns

willingly and keeps his rhythm and balance on the corner.

The rider must be careful that he does not pull back on the corner and so stop the forward movement. An open inside rein can guide the horse round while the outside rein controls the shoulder. The outside leg brings the quarters round and, along with the inside leg, maintains the impulsion. Rhythm is the key word - if the horse keeps the rhythm, he will have kept this balance and not lost impulsion.

The rider can now ask the horse to turn from the other way. If the horse resists as he turns, rather than become stiff in the hand, try giving and taking and opening the hand in a more exaggerated way to guide the horse round. Once the horse turns off both reins, he can be asked to complete the exercise.

Two-fence exercise

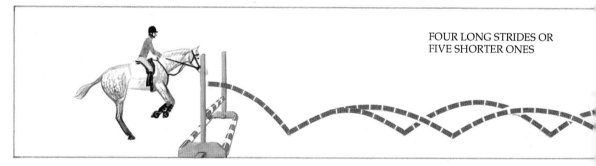

FOUR LONG STRIDES OR FIVE SHORTER ONES

The final exercise is designed to help horse and rider to keep rhythm, balance and impulsion between fences. It also gives the rider good practice in judging his horse's stride and rhythm.

Two fences set at 18m (60ft) apart and with ground lines on both sides so that they can be jumped from either way, present the horse with a distance where he can take either four long strides or five short ones. A pony, having a much

shorter stride, can take as many as he chooses. It is much easier for a short-striding horse or pony to alter his stride than it is for a long-striding animal.

Initially, with small fences, the horse will find five strides quite comfortable. As the fences get bigger, so the horse will have more of an option of taking only four strides. The pace of the canter and the way he jumps in over the first part will determine whether four or five

strides are suitable. Sometimes, five strides may seem rather awkward and four too long. For this reason, it is best to use upright fences rather than parallels because they are more forgiving if the horse does make a mistake. Landing on the back pole of a parallel can injure a horse's back and shake his confidence.

Whenever a horse or pony has to alter the stride pattern, it it imperative that he does not lose rhythm. Any loss of rhythm indicates a lack of impulsion and balance. All work done on the flat should be geared towards the horse being able to lengthen and shorten his stride without losing rhythm or balance. These two fences will be proof that the flatwork has been correctly undertaken. They should be jumped off either rein.

Final thoughts

The more you perfect the skill of jumping and presenting the horse at his fences with rhythm, balance and impulsion, the more successful you will be, whether negotiating show jumps or cross-country fences.

Remember, never jump the same grid too often, otherwise your horse will become bored and tired. Grids should only be used once or twice a week. Keep the work varied and avoid over-jumping your horse.

Do not jump your horse on bad ground - it may cause injury and make him lose enthusiasm for his work.

Grids are suppling exercises and should work hand in hand with flatwork. However, they are a means to an end and it is important also to jump single fences from canter. It is, after all, from canter that the horse has to jump in competition - there are no placing poles then!

You must practise angled jumping and jumping from a variety of paces over a variety of different distances at home. It is unfair suddenly to present a horse with a complex question in a competition. He must be used to jumping miniature versions of all competition problems at home.

A secure seat is important to enable you to keep not only your own balance but also that of your horse. You must be in the correct position to be able to recover from a mistake - inevitable when going cross-country.

Practice makes perfect, but not without hard work and effort. Persevere with achieving a correct position - it will pay off!